The Complete IC Diet Cookbook

Over 70 delicious recipes free of gluten, dairy, and refined sugar

Elisabeth Yaotani & Brianne Thornton, MS, RD

Copyright November 2019
All rights reserved
ISBN:

No part of this publication may be reproduced or transmitted in any form or by any means, electronic or mechanical, including photocopy, recordings, or any information storage and retrieval system, without permission in writing from its authors.

This book is not to represented as an alternative to, or substitute for, the consultation of professional physicians or nutritionists. Instead, it serves as an additional resource, providing information that will enable you to make informed decisions. All material in The Complete IC Diet Cookbook is for informational purposes only and may not be construed as medical advice. It is always best to discuss any health-related issue with a medical professional first.

Photography by Alexia Magallanes
and Stock Adobe

To the IC Community

We are in this together!

Nourishing Your Body

BREAKFAST // 16

SMOOTHIES & JUICES // 23

BEVERAGES // 28

BREADS // 34

SOUPS // 38

HUMMUS // 51

SALADS // 56

MAIN COURSES // 69

FISH // 85

SIDES // 89

SWEETS // 101

IC DIET PROTOCOL
SUPPLEMENTS & HERBS
TEAS FOR WELLNESS

ABOUT THE AUTHORS

Elisabeth Yaotani

At the age of 29, I was diagnosed with interstitial cystitis, a painful bladder syndrome with no hope of a cure. The prospect of living the rest of my life in chronic pain was devastating, and my quality of life quickly started to diminish.

Over the next decade, I struggled to make life as normal as possible for my three children and husband. Through it all, I continued to suffer with daily pain that was at times debilitating and experience a host of other symptoms that ranged from migraines and brain fog to candida overgrowth, GI issues, hives, and allergies. Conventional medicine offered me symptom management at best. At worst, I was left fighting my body on a daily basis.

I found the answer in alternative medicine. Functional medicine taught me that healing begins with your fork. Changing my diet brought significant improvement to my health. After 11 years of suffering, it took just 12 months of working to heal my gut through food, lifestyle, and proper supplementation to finally see results. Within one year, I had sent my IC into remission.

Today, by eliminating my intake of inflammatory foods like gluten, conventional dairy, and refined sugars, I am more in control of my health than ever before. After the release of my book How I Got My Life Back; My Journey with Interstitial Cystitis, I realized that there exists a great need for a cookbook that provides bladder friendly recipes. Integrative and functional nutritionist Brianne Thornton and I collaborated to bring you a cookbook that we believe will provide you with whole nutrient-dense meals that you can feel good about. Together, we wanted to offer healthy food that also tasted delicious. These recipes take the fear out of making the switch to clean eating. It can be simple, life changing, and mouth-watering too! Bon appetit.

ABOUT THE AUTHORS

Brianne Thornton MS, RD

As a child, I was active and participated in a variety of sports, but my diet was far from nourishing. Unfortunately, I regularly had access to and consumed candy, chips, soda, and ice cream, and as a result, I was fairly overweight. When I had difficulty breathing while playing sports, I went to the doctor only to find out that I did not have sports induced asthma, but acid reflux. I also had terrible seasonal allergies and an extreme reaction whenever I entered a home with cats. Up until 12 years ago, I had to take medication for acid reflux and allergies daily or I was miserable.

When I joined the high school swim team, my coach stressed the importance of nutrition for athletic performance, and I began changing my diet by cutting out all of the junk food I was addicted to. After I saw a dramatic improvement in my times, I realized first-hand the powerful influence diet has on our life and our health. As I continued to move toward a whole food, plant-based diet, and mindful eating, I noticed I no longer suffered from symptoms of acid reflux, and my allergies virtually disappeared (allowing me to adopt the sweetest cat). This experience not only encouraged me to fuel and nourish my body with quality food, but it led me to pursue a career as a dietitian.

After working as a dietitian for a couple of years, I found I wasn't able to provide the care I knew my patients needed. Yes, I could educate them on a diet for diabetes or heart disease, but those with conditions like interstitial cystitis needed something more. This led me to pursue a Master of Science (MS) in Integrative and Functional Nutrition, which provided training on how to identify and remove barriers that prevent healing and address the underlying cause of illness. This training has given me the knowledge and skills necessary to provide whole-person, individualized care and promote true healing in those who are often left without answers from traditional medicine.

I am forever grateful Elisabeth and I crossed paths, and that she invited me to join her mission to serve others suffering from IC. Our work with IC Wellness is so fulfilling because we are empowering our community to take control of their health instead of succumbing to the idea that they are powerless in this journey. This cookbook is a labor of love founded on our passion to break down the barriers to wellness, and we could not be more excited to share these delicious, wholesome recipes with you.

INTRODUCTION

Why We Eat Clean

The best approach to our health gets to the root of the problem: removing the culprits that set off our immune system and boosting those sources that strengthen it. The more research is done into diseases, the more we see that inflammation is almost always a leading cause. When we pay attention to diet and lifestyle triggers, we can strengthen our immune system, restoring vitality and health.

Eating clean is all about taking care of our body, mind, and soul. It means centering our diets around the best and healthiest options, including whole organic foods (think natural) and lots of fresh fruits and vegetables. It also means staying away from processed and refined foods, including refined sugars, which are proven to undermine health.

While eating clean is a good idea for all of us, there still exist unique trigger foods that can cause different kinds of inflammation in different individuals. That's why it's important to get to know your body and tailor your diet accordingly. That's also why, in this cookbook, we've chosen not to include any recipes with two of the most problematic foods for many people: gluten and refined sugar. Gluten and sugar play a major role in illness, so by removing it from our diets and choosing to eat clean, we believe one can lay the foundation for better health.

For those who are intolerant to dairy (lactose or casein), you will note that certain recipes call for raw butter or ghee. We made the decision to use raw butter or Ghee selectively due to its health benefits. However, feel free to omit it, or if you want to use a substitute, applesauce or coconut oil will make for an equally delicious meal.

It's important for all of us to listen to what our bodies are telling us and make the necessary changes as we go. Congratulations on beginning your journey to a healthier you!

Our Impression of the "Traditional" IC Diet

We believe that the traditional IC Diet was developed with the best of intention using the best available information at the time. The traditional IC diet is based on a questionnaire, which Drs. Moldwin and Shorter used to survey 104 IC patients. Each patient was asked how a list of 175 different foods affected their symptoms. As you have likely read, they found that the most bothersome foods for IC patients to be

- Caffeinated and decaffeinated coffee and tea
- Citrus fruits and juices
- Alcoholic beverages
- Carbonated beverages
- Tomatoes
- Foods containing hot peppers
- Certain artificial sweeteners
- Pineapple/pineapple juice
- Cranberry juice
- Vinegar
- Pickled herring

While many people with IC find that their symptoms correlate with these foods, we now know that identifying individual food intolerances can be somewhat tricky. This is due impart to IC/PBS being a chronic inflammatory condition, and correlation does not always imply causation. There is also a strong connection between the fear and stress surrounding foods/eating and bladder symptoms. Additionally, food sensitivities can be much trickier to discover because they trigger an IgG response, which can take up to three days or 72 hours to take effect. For many with IC/PBS, by the time a response has made itself known, it's almost impossible to go back through the list of everything you ate and drank in the last three days, let alone every product you have used, and identify the offender.

Lastly, many of the foods on the traditional IC Diet that have been listed as "bladder friendly" should not be included in any healthy diet for healing, as these foods cause inflammation and undermine health. These foods include milkshakes, ice cream, cake, frosting, pie, cheesecake, licorice candy, pastries, and white sugar. Nearly every person who comes to IC Wellness for support has tried to follow the traditional IC Diet with little to no progress in finding true healing. Instead, many restrict their diet even further to manage their symptoms and end up eating the same foods every day, which increases the risk of developing new food sensitivities.

While diet alone is often not the root cause of IC/PBS, it can contribute to inflammation and be a barrier to healing. Clean eating and an anti-inflammatory diet will complement other therapies that address the root cause of IC/PBS, which is the inspiration of this cookbook. We have found that once someone has healed and their IC/PBS is in remission, the foods listed in the traditional IC diet are no longer triggers for their symptoms, as long as they maintain a clean diet in addition to self-care and stress management.

Personalized Nutrition

This cookbook provides IC friendly recipes that eliminate common trigger foods for those with IC/PBS. Unfortunately, it is not possible to ensure these recipes are appropriate for every single person who opens it. For each chronic disease, there are specific foods that a person should choose and certain foods they should avoid. With multiple chronic diseases, the list of restrictions grows. If you have other conditions in addition to IC/PBS, it is important to work with your provider and an experienced nutritionist to develop a personalized diet that addresses your specific needs. To determine your unique food triggers, you could consider an elimination diet, such as a low histamine or low oxalate diet, as research has found foods high in these compounds can contribute to IC/PBS symptoms. A reliable and accurate way to identify which foods and food chemicals are triggering inflammation in your body is to complete the MRT food sensitivity test and work with a trained registered dietitian to complete the LEAP diet based on your results.

Once you understand your unique nutrition needs, you can modify the recipes in this book to make them fit your individualized diet.

How to use this cookbook

We have provided a substitution list which you can reference for each recipe in this book, allowing you to customize it to your specific needs. You may also choose to omit ingredients if you prefer. Don't be afraid to try new foods and be encouraged that as inflammation in the bladder subsides, you will likely be able to tolerate foods like oranges, grapefruit, seasonings and spices. Remember to be patient and don't be afraid to fail.

We understand monetary restraints, so if you cannot afford to buy organic, we encourage you to do the best you can. Start out by replacing one meal a day with a recipe from this book. You do not have to go into your cupboard and throw everything away if you do not have the means to replace it all with healthier options. Use what you have and when it runs out seek to replace it, if you can. If you cannot afford to buy organic produce, be sure to check the EWG's Dirty Dozen list, as these foods have higher levels of pesticide residue and you will want to avoid them.

Why we chose to include lemon in some of our recipes

We think of lemon as acidic because of the pH before digestion; however, it actually depends on the acidic or alkaline byproducts created once the food is digested and processed by your body. Vegetables and fruits, such as lemon, are high in alkaline nutrients like potassium, calcium and magnesium. Therefore, they help reduce the amount of acid that the kidneys must filter. Those with IC/PBS can often tolerate lemon zest and lemon oil as substitutes. For those with mild IC/PBS, you can consider trying Meyer lemons, as these are less acidic.

What to Eat

- **Bacon,** that is organic, pasture-raised, and nitrate-free
- **Bone Broth,** make your own or buy organic
- **Butter,** such as imported (Irish), raw, ghee, coconut butter
- **Cheese** (if tolerated), such as feta (sheep or goat), goat, raw, and sheep milk cheese, vegan cheese
- **Eggs** from organic free-range chickens
- **Flours,** such as nut flours, coconut flour, gluten-free oat, buckwheat, cassava, chickpea, *rice, *sprouted corn, *sprouted oat, and teff
- **Fish** that are low-mercury and wild-caught
- **Fruits** that are organic
- **Grains,** such as amaranth, buckwheat, millet (organic, gluten-free), polenta, quinoa (non-GMO), sprouted sorghum, and teff
- **Healthy fats,** such as avocado, olive, coconut, walnut, flaxseed, sesame, and pumpkin
- **Meat,** that is 100% grass-fed, grass-finished, pasture-raised, and/or organic
- **Milk,** including organic nut, rice, coconut, oat, raw, goat, and sheep's milk
- **Nuts,** such as walnuts, almonds, cashews, pumpkin, pine, and macadamia. Soak in filtered water for 24 hours beforehand then rinse.
- **Pasta,** such as egg noodles, gluten-free, rice noodles, zucchini or spaghetti squash
- **Poultry,** that is organic and free-range
- **Rice,** including sprouted organic and cauliflower rice
- **Salt,** including sea salt, Himalayan pink salt, and kosher salt
- **Sweeteners,** including raw honey, coconut palm sugar, stevia, 100% maple syrup, blackstrap molasses, Manuka honey, Medjool dates, and monk fruit
- **Vegetables** that are organic

Product Recommendations for Clean Eating

Acai – Sambazon Organic Pure Unsweetened Acai

All-Purpose Flour – Bob's Red Mill gluten-free

Almond milk – Califia Farms almond milk

Avocado oil – Bella Vado organic extra virgin

Bacon – Applewood organic bacon

Baking powder – Thrive Market

Baking soda – Thrive Market

Bone broth – Butcher's Bone Broth, Pressery Bone Broth

Bread – Canyon Bakehouse Ancient Grains, gluten-free

Butter – Kerrygold, Thrive Market Organic Ghee, Miyoko's Cultured Vegan Butter

Carob – Terrasoul Superfoods Organic Carob Powder

Cashew milk – Forager Project cashew milk

Cheese – Treeline or Treenut cheese

Coconut (raw) – Let's Do Organic 100% unsweetened organic coconut flakes

Coconut flour – Bob's Red Mill

Coconut milk – So Delicious organic unsweetened coconut milk

Coconut oil – Trader Joe's organic virgin coconut oil

Cooking spray – Primal Kitchen Avocado Oil Spray

Corn starch – Thrive Market Organic Corn Starch or Organic Arrowroot powder

Cream Cheese – Kite Hill Plain Almond Milk cream cheese

Deli meat – Applegate organic, nitrate-free

Feta cheese – Pastures of Eden sheep's milk

Gelatin – Great Lakes Porcine Gelatin

Macadamia nut milk – Milkadamia unsweetened

Maple syrup – 365 Everyday Value organic grade A

Mayo – Primal Kitchen Mayo Avocado Oil

Meat – Butcher Box or Grass Roots Coop

Nut butter – Barney Almond Butter, Artisana Organics, NuttZo 7 Nut & Seed Butter

Oat flour – Bob's Red Mill oat flour, gluten-free

Oat milk – Thrive Market Organic Oat Beverage

Olive oil – La Tourangelle 100% organic extra virgin olive oil

Parchment paper – IF YOU CARE unbleached parchment baking paper

Rice milk – Thrive Market organic rice

Ricotta cheese – Kite Hill

Salt – Morton Kosher Salt

Shortening – Nutiva Shortening

Soy Sauce – San-J Organic Tamari or Coconut Secret coconut aminos

Spices – Simply Organic

Sweeteners – Lakanto Monkfruit sweetener, Microingredients Pure Organic stevia, Nutiva organic coconut sugar

Vanilla – Simply Organic Madagascar vanilla extract

Walnut milk – Elmhurst milked walnuts

Yogurt – Kite Hill Plain Yogurt, Nancy's Probiotic Oat Milk, Forager Project

Ingredient Substitution List

Apple – pear
Avocado – hummus, nut butter, banana, chia seeds, pesto, feta, chayote squash, pureed (peas, broccoli, or asparagus)
Banana – Medjool dates, ½ cup apple sauce, coconut cream, avocado, oats, frozen fruit
Bread – lettuce, coconut wraps, Watusee organic chickpea crumbs
Butter – ghee, oil, pumpkin puree, apple sauce, almond or coconut butter, plant-based butter
Carob powder – Almond powder
Carrot – parsnip, beets, asparagus
Cashew Cultured Beverage – cashew milk
Chickpeas – Tiger nuts, riced cauliflower, canned tuna
Eggs – Ener-G replacer, 1 tbsp. chia or ground flaxseed with 3 tbsp. water (for baking), or organic extra firm tofu (for breakfast recipes)
Feta cheese – vegan cheese, nut-based
Flour – cassava, tiger nut, oat, almond, coconut, all-purpose gluten-free
Garlic – garlic infused oil (4 garlic cloves simmered in oil for 30 minutes then stored for 1 month)
Lemon juice (Meyer lemons are less acidic) – lemon extract (use 1/3 of the volume and add water for the other 2/3 of the volume), lemon zest, lemon oil, juice from a green apple
Lentils – split pea, yellow pea, green pea, and quinoa
Mango – peach
Milk – almond, organic soy, organic rice, coconut, oat, cashew, macadamia, hemp, quinoa
Monk fruit – coconut sugar
Oil – coconut, walnut, olive, pumpkin
Onion – chives, leeks (white part only), shallots, green onions
Potato – turnip, cauliflower rice, rutabaga
Pumpkin – acorn squash, butternut squash, sweet potato
Soy Sauce – coconut aminos, fish sauce, Bragg Liquid Aminos
Spinach – kale, chard, dandelions, arugula, Romaine lettuce, watercress, collard
Strawberries – raspberries, blackberries, blueberries, boysenberries, olallieberries
Turmeric – fresh turmeric, ginger, saffron, paprika, cumin
Vinegar – organic apple juice, lemon juice, omit

Meal Prepping

Meal prepping makes eating healthy much easier because everything is ready to grab and go. When it's not convenient, it's easy to slip into old habits like grabbing prepackaged snacks, throwing a frozen meal in the microwave, or stopping somewhere on the way to work and on the way home.

Here are some key meal prep tips:

1. **Find recipes**. This cookbook provides you with the foundation for IC friendly recipes. If you have any traditional family favorites with trigger foods, you can use the substitution list to make it IC friendly.
2. **Make a meal plan**. Yes, I literally make a menu with meal options for the week. It's important to anticipate any dinner plans for the week and allow for a night or two of leftovers (or plan to bring those for lunch instead).
3. **Set aside time**. While it's more efficient to prep everything at once, you'll want to give yourself a couple of hours to chop and sort into containers (Also, make sure you have appropriate containers – I love mason jars and glass Pyrex).
4. **Look for short cuts**. If you know you don't have a couple of hours to meal prep, try buying already prepped items like pre-riced cauliflower or washed veggies.
5. **Batch cook**. If you don't have 30 minutes after work to bake chicken or fish, do it all on meal prep day and use it over the next 3 days.
6. **Utilize small appliances**. Gadgets like a crockpot, Instapot or air fryer can help you prep meals quickly and efficiently instead of spending hours slaving away in the kitchen.
7. **Always prep breakfast**. When you're running late in the morning, the last thing you have time for is to cook breakfast, and lack of planning can lead to you grabbing something less healthy on the run.

Shopping on a Budget

1. Look in your pantry to see what you already have and cross it off your grocery list. This will not only help keep your grocery total low but will prevent having extra food spoil before you can use it.
2. Try looking at the store ad for sales and coupons before you go. While it may take trips to different stores, this can help keep your grocery total low.
3. Eat a snack before you go. If you go to the store hungry, you are more likely to buy items not on your list and spend more.
4. Bring your grocery list to the store and try to stick to it. This will not only keep your grocery total low but will also help you avoid buying foods with pro-inflammatory ingredients.
5. Bring a pen to the store and cross off items as you go to make sure you don't miss any ingredients.
6. Consider buying in bulk or buying the larger container of the item you need, as the cost per ounce generally is lower for these items. If the store doesn't provide you the cost per ounce, simply divide the total cost by the volume to compare products.
7. Consider shopping at the farmer's market, trying services like Imperfect Produce, or growing your own produce! When the produce is not in season, buying frozen produce can help to keep the cost low.

Remember to grab your reusable grocery bags!

Note – If grocery shopping is not your favorite or is overwhelming, try to go in the off hours (very early in the morning or later at night) so it is not so busy.

Anti-inflammatory Foods

One of the best ways to incorporate in anti-inflammatory foods is to focus on whole foods that are as close to their natural state and the least processed as possible. One eating pattern well known for focusing on anti-inflammatory foods is the Mediterranean diet, which incorporates:

1. **Fruits**: especially blueberries, raspberries, black plums, red grapes, sweet cherries, apples, pears
2. **Vegetables**: especially kale, spinach, Brussels sprouts, broccoli, red cabbage
3. **Nuts & seeds**: especially walnuts, almonds, pecans, flaxseeds, chia seeds
4. **Whole grains**: amaranth, quinoa, buckwheat, millet, brown rice, wild rice, oats.
5. **Fish**: Especially salmon, tuna, mackerel
6. **Legumes**: lentils, chickpeas, beans
7. **Healthy oils/fats**: especially extra virgin olive oil, avocado oil, avocados, Salmon
8. **Spices**: such as turmeric, ginger, cinnamon, cloves, sage, cumin, rosemary
9. **Teas**: especially, Turmeric and Ginger

Many of these foods are high in vitamins, such as vitamins A, C, and E, minerals, such as magnesium and various phytonutrients such as carotenoids and anthocyanins, which act as antioxidants. The general recommendation is for 2 cups of fruit and 2 cups of vegetables per day, but the more the better!

In addition to anti-inflammatory foods, there are a variety of other lifestyle factors that can help lower inflammation. It is important to avoid smoking and limit alcohol intake, as these can introduce toxins that contribute to inflammation. Adequate exercise, with the goal of at least 150 minutes per week and adequate sleep, with the goal of 7-9 hours per night, has also been found to lower levels of inflammation in our body. Finally, managing stress through yoga, tai chi, meditation, breathing exercises, mindfulness-based stress reduction, or progressive muscle relaxation is essential to lowering inflammation.

IC Friendly Snack Ideas

Apple with almond butter
Hummus with veggies
A handful of almonds
Kale chips
Roasted chickpeas
Handful of trial mix
Rice cake with almond butter
Avocado toast
Smoothie
Chia pudding
Overnight oats
Cassava chips
Organic air popped popcorn with sea salt and butter
Cup of berries
Zucchini muffin
Baked sweet potato
Butternut squash fries
Edamame
Granola bar
Paleo Protein Bar
Fruit salad
Coconut yogurt with granola or fruit
Guacamole and organic corn tortilla chips
Clean energy bites
Dried mango slices
Homemade popsicles
Bone broth
Baked sweet potato chips
Cucumber slices topped with feta cheese and seasoned with paprika
Clean Berry Parfait (nondairy)
Golden latte
Clean jerky

Clean Products

Air Purifiers: GermGuardian

Bed linens: No Feathers Please organic cotton

Body Moisture: Beautycounter

Body wash: Beautycounter

Cleaning products: GreenShield Organic

Cookware: GreenPan

Deodorant: Primally Pure, Humankind

Dishwasher liquid: Planet Ultra

Feminine hygiene products: LOLA, Cora

Haircare: Beautycounter Repair & Nourish Shampoo

Laundry detergent: 365 Everyday Value Lavender

Makeup: Beauty Counter, W311 People

Nail polish: butter London, 100% Pure

Shower head: Sonaki Vitamin C Inline Shower

Skincare: Beautycounter

Sunscreen: Beautycounter

Toothpaste: Revitin's prebiotic toothpaste

Water pitcher: Propur Water Filter Pitcher

Breakfast

Pumpkin Paleo Pancakes
Serves 2-3

½ cup organic pumpkin
3 tablespoons Cashew or Coconut Unsweetened Cultured Beverage
4 organic eggs
1 teaspoon organic vanilla extract
1 teaspoon cinnamon
¼ cup almond or coconut flour
dash of nutmeg
1/8 teaspoon Himalayan salt
¼ teaspoon baking soda
½ teaspoon pumpkin spice
¼ to ½ cup carob chocolate chips (optional)
1 tablespoon ghee or coconut oil

In a medium sized bowl, whisk together the pumpkin, milk (can use cashew milk), eggs, vanilla, cinnamon, flour, nutmeg, salt, baking soda, and pumpkin spice. Once mixed, you can fold in the carob chips if desired. Heat griddle or flat pan over medium heat and then grease pan with ghee or coconut oil. Spoon ¼ cup of batter onto the pan. Cook 2-3 minutes and then flip cooking for another 2-3 minutes. Serve hot with maple syrup and fresh fruit if desired.

Whipped Eggs & Sardines
Serves 1

2 eggs, whisked
1 cup broccoli floret
½ cup spinach, kale, or chard
1 green onion, diced
1 asparagus, chopped into ½ inch pieces
2 teaspoons ghee (see substitution list)
1 can wild-caught sardines in water, drained
fresh chives
salt and pepper to taste

In a nonstick skillet, melt 1 teaspoon ghee over medium-low heat. Add broccoli, spinach, onion, and asparagus and sauté for 4-5 minutes. Add in eggs and season with salt and pepper. Continue cooking for another 4 minutes or until eggs are cooked and remove from heat and place on a plate.

Return pan to stove and add 1-teaspoon ghee, allowing it to melt over medium heat. Add desired number of sardines to pan and sauté for 2 minutes. Place sardines on top of eggs and sprinkle with chives. You can also top with half an avocado or a handful of microgreens.

Overnight Oats

Serves 1

½ cup oats
¾ cup unsweetened nut milk
1 tablespoon chia seeds or ground flaxseed
1 tablespoon maple syrup or honey
Optional: pinch of stevia

Flavor Options

Almond Joy: 2 tablespoons carob chips, 2 tablespoons untreated organic shredded coconut, 2 tablespoons slivered almonds
Apple Cinnamon: Add ½ teaspoon cinnamon, 1 apple diced, 2 tablespoons almond butter
Carrot Cake: 1/3 cup finely shredded carrot, ½ teaspoon cinnamon, 2 tablespoons almond butter, 2 tablespoons raisins, 1 tablespoon chopped walnuts, 2 tablespoons unsweetened shredded coconut, 1 teaspoon vanilla extract
Pumpkin Pie: ½ cup canned pumpkin (only use ½ cup milk), ¼ teaspoon cinnamon, 2 tablespoons slivered almonds
Strawberries & Cream: ½ cup sliced strawberries, use coconut milk, 3 tablespoons hemp seed

Add all ingredients to a glass container or mason jar. Mix with a spoon (or put a lid on the container and shake well), cover and put in the fridge overnight. The next morning, you can heat it up a bit or enjoy cold!

Note: You can meal prep by making 3 servings at a time

Avocado Toast

Serves 1

1 slice of bread
½ ripe avocado, thinly sliced
1 tablespoon hummus (page 49)
1 handful of microgreens
1 egg. You can boil, scramble, fry, or poach
salt and pepper to taste
dash of garlic salt (optional)
olive oil
dash of lemon
Everything but the Bagel Seasoning

Heat a non-stick skillet over low heat. Drizzle with oil to coat the bottom of the pan. Gently crack the egg into the skillet and cook to your liking. Season the egg with salt and pepper. Next, toast the bread. Spread hummus on toast, then using a fork gently mash the avocado on top of the hummus. Place egg over avocado and top with microgreens and lightly drizzle olive oil over the greens and add a dash of lemon. Season with Everything but the Bagel Seasoning.

Sweet Potato Hash

Serves 2-4

1 teaspoon ghee (see substitution list)
1 large sweet potato, unpeeled and washed cut into ½ inch pieces
1 cup celery root, peeled and cut into ½ inch pieces
2 cups butternut squash, cut into ½ inch pieces
4 slices organic pasture-raised bacon, chopped
½ sweet onion, finely chopped
1 clove garlic, minced
1/8 teaspoon smoked or regular paprika
1/8 teaspoon garlic powder
1 teaspoon thyme
4 large eggs
1 tablespoon minced chives
salt and pepper to taste

In cast iron or nonstick skillet heat 1 teaspoon of ghee. Add potato, celery, squash, onion, garlic, and bacon. Sauté over medium-high heat. Season with paprika, garlic powder, and thyme and cook until vegetables are tender about 10 minutes (make sure to stir 3-4 times while cooking). Add salt and pepper to taste and transfer hash to a bowl.

Wipe skillet with a paper towel if needed, but make sure to leave enough grease to cover bottom of pan (add ghee if needed so that the eggs don't stick to the pan). Crack eggs into pan and then season with salt and pepper. Let cook 2-3 minutes or until whites are cooked but make sure the yolk is still runny. Meanwhile, divide hash between 2-4 plates. Remove eggs from skillet and place on top of the hash. Sprinkle with chives and serve.

Smoothies & Juices

Mango Smoothie

1 mango or 1 large peach
1 cup coconut milk
1 cup spinach
1 tablespoon flaxseed
1 teaspoon cinnamon
1 teaspoon vanilla
1 scoop collagen powder

Pear Mango Smoothie

1 small pear
1 small mango or peach
1 cup kale or spinach
1 tablespoon almond butter
1 ½ cups coconut water

Peaches and Cream Smoothie

1 peach
1 cup unsweetened nut milk
½ cup nut-based yogurt
1 tablespoon honey
1 teaspoon cinnamon
1 scoop collagen

Pumpkin Smoothie

1 ½ cups unsweetened nut milk
A handful of spinach
1/3 cup organic pumpkin puree
¼ cup acai (optional)
½ banana
4 frozen strawberries
½ teaspoon cinnamon
½ teaspoon vanilla
2 tablespoons pecans

Double Berry Smoothie

1 cup coconut water
A handful of spinach, kale, or mixed greens
5 blackberries
¼ cup blueberries
1 cup peach

Cinnamon Pear Smoothie

1 cup unsweetened almond milk
½ organic pear
1 teaspoon ground flaxseed
1 tablespoon almond butter
½ banana
¼ teaspoon cinnamon
½ cup berry of choice
½ cup spinach
1 scoop collagen powder
¼ cup acai

Carrot and Beet Juice

1 beet
3 carrots
1 celery
2 apples or pears, core and seeds removed
1 cucumber

Go Green Juice

1 cup spinach or kale
4 celery stalks
1/3 cup cilantro
1-inch piece of ginger, peeled 1 cucumber

Sweet Greens Juice

1 Gala apple, core and seeds removed
1 pear, core and seeds removed
2 cups spinach, kale, or chard
½ cup parsley
1 cucumber
1 stalk celery

Beverages

Pumpkin Spice Latte
Serves 1

1 tea bag Decaf Chai Spice
½ cup coconut milk
1 tablespoon 100% pure maple syrup
2 tablespoons pumpkin puree
½ teaspoon vanilla
¼ teaspoon pumpkin spice
coconut whip cream (optional)
dash of cinnamon

In a small pot, bring water to a low boil and steep tea bag for 3 minutes and then discard tea bag. Add milk, syrup, pumpkin, vanilla, and pumpkin spice and whisk until blended. Turn off heat and pour into a mug. Top with coconut whip cream and a dash of cinnamon.

Golden Milk Latte

Serves 1

1 cup unsweetened nut milk
1 teaspoon 100% pure maple syrup or honey
¼ teaspoon ground turmeric
pinch of black pepper
⅛ teaspoon ground cinnamon or 1 cinnamon stick
¼ teaspoon pure vanilla extract
½ teaspoon coconut oil

Heat milk in a saucepan over low heat on the stovetop (do not boil) and stir continuously. Add remaining ingredients and let heat for 1 minute. Remove from stove and use a hand blender to mix well and froth. Pour into your favorite ceramic mug and enjoy!

Coconut Milk Latte
Serves 1

16 ounces' hot water
1 bag of tea (corn silk, ginger, marshmallow root, licorice)
¼ cup canned coconut milk
dash of cinnamon
1 scoop collagen powder (optional)
¼ teaspoon agave syrup

Heat coconut milk in a saucepan over medium heat and allow to lightly boil for 2 minutes. Meanwhile, in a mug steep tea bag in hot water for 5 minutes. Remove tea bag and pour in coconut milk. Stir in collagen powder, sweeten with agave syrup, and finish with a dash of cinnamon.

Nut Milk

2 cups nuts (raw macadamia, almond, cashew, walnut)
6 cups filtered water
2 pinches Himalayan salt
1 teaspoon vanilla extract
Sweetener: 2 pitted Medjool dates

Place 1 cup of nuts in a glass bowl and add 2 cups of water or enough water to cover them. Soak nuts in water for 24 to 48 hours. After 24 to 48 hours, drain and rinse. Place nuts in blender and add 4 cups of filtered water. Blend for 2 minutes. Using a nut milk bag, strain the milk through the bag making sure to squeeze the bag from top down. Add stevia, vanilla, and salt to milk and stir. If sweetening with dates, return the milk to the blender and add dates. Blend until smooth. Place in mason jar and cover tightly with lid and refrigerate until chilled. You can store the milk in the fridge for up to 5 days.

Breads

Pumpkin Pie Paleo Muffins
Makes 12

1 cup organic pumpkin puree
2 eggs
¼ canned coconut milk
1 ½ cups almond flour
½ teaspoon salt
¼ teaspoon baking soda
¼ teaspoon baking powder
1 teaspoon cinnamon
½ teaspoon nutmeg
1 teaspoon vanilla
3 tablespoons 100% pure maple syrup
½ cup monk fruit

Heat oven to 350°F and line muffin tin. Mix all ingredients together in a bowl. Fill 12 muffin tins and bake for 35 minutes or until cooked through. Let cool.

Zucchini Bread
Makes 12

1 ¼ cups almond flour
1 ½ cups zucchini, shredded
2 eggs
¼ cup coconut oil
1 ½ teaspoons vanilla
1 teaspoon baking soda
½ teaspoon salt
1 ¼ teaspoon cinnamon
¼ teaspoon nutmeg
2 tablespoons honey
½ cup monk fruit

Heat oven to 350°F and line muffins tins. Mix all ingredients together with a whisk until blended. Fill each muffin tin with about 1/4 cup batter and bake for 30 minutes.

Soups

Minestrone Soup

Serves 6

2 tablespoons avocado oil
1 sweet onion, chopped
2 cloves garlic, minced
2 cups celery, chopped
4 carrots, sliced
1 cup organic kidney beans, rinsed
2 cups green beans cut into ½ inch pieces
2 zucchinis, chopped
½ yellow bell pepper, chopped
½ beet (white), peeled and chopped
2 cups spinach
½ cup sprouted rice, cooked
5 cups bone broth, chicken
1 tablespoon oregano
3 tablespoons fresh basil, sliced
salt and pepper to taste

Heat stockpot over medium-low heat; add oil and sauté onion for 2 minutes. Add garlic, celery, and carrots and sauté for another 2 minutes. Add broth and bring to a boil. Reduce heat to low and add beans, green beans, zucchini, bell pepper, beet, spinach, oregano, and basil. Salt and pepper to taste. Simmer for 40 minutes (or until veggies are tender). Add rice and continue cooking for another 5 minutes. Ladle soup into individual serving bowls and top with additional fresh basil if desired.

Zucchini-Basil Soup

Serves 4

2 zucchinis, slice in half and chop
2 tablespoons shallot, minced
2 cloves garlic, minced
2 cups cauliflower
2 cups bone broth, chicken
1 cup canned coconut milk
2 tablespoons avocado oil
½ cup basil
½ tablespoon salt
pepper to taste
nutmeg to garnish

Over medium heat add oil to a large pan and sauté shallots, zucchini, garlic, and cauliflower. Season with salt and let cook 6-7 minutes. Add broth and reduce heat to low. Let simmer for 15 minutes. Turn off heat and let cool for 10 minutes. Pour into a blender and add basil and coconut milk (I use a BlendTec, but depending on the size of your blender, you may need to make it in two batches), and blend until smooth. Salt and pepper to taste. When serving garnish with nutmeg.

Mushroom Lentil Stew
Serves 2

1 tablespoon extra-virgin olive oil or avocado oil
1 clove garlic, minced
1 cup mushroom, sliced
1 stalk celery, diced
1 carrot, diced
3 cups low sodium vegetable broth
2 tablespoons dried Italian Seasoning
1 tablespoon coconut aminos
1 cup lentil (soak for 3 to 12 hours beforehand then rinse)
a handful of spinach or chard
½ cup unsweetened nut milk
1 tablespoon Bragg's organic apple cider vinegar (optional)

Sauté garlic in oil until lightly browned. Add mushrooms and cook until browned. Add celery and carrots, cook for 5 minutes until soft. Add vegetable broth, lentils, coconut aminos, and seasoning then bring to a boil. Reduce heat, cover, and simmer for 30 minutes until lentils are cooked. Add spinach, milk, and vinegar, stir to combine and serve.

Meatball Soup

Serves 4

1 pound organic ground turkey
2 eggs, beaten
2 slices of bread, torn into pieces (or substitute with 1 cup Watusee organic chickpea crumbs)
2 cloves garlic, minced
½ teaspoon fresh parsley, chopped
1 ½ teaspoons kosher salt
1/8 teaspoon pepper
1/8 teaspoon nutmeg
2 tablespoons avocado oil
8 cups bone broth, chicken
a handful of spinach or chard (optional)

In a bowl, use your hand to mix together the turkey, eggs, garlic, parsley, salt, pepper, and nutmeg. Add bread and mix lightly. Divide into 12 meatballs. In large skillet heat oil over medium to low heat. Cook the meatballs making sure to turn every few minutes so that they do not burn. Cook for 10 minutes or until cooked. Line a plate with a paper towel and transfer meatballs to plate. Continue cooking batches of meatballs.

In a pot, add bone broth and bring to a low boil. If using spinach or chard, add to pot and allow to boil for 3 minutes. Add in cooked meatballs and heat for 2 minutes. Remove pot from the stove and serve.

Homemade Tortilla Soup

Serves 6

1 tablespoon avocado oil
1 sweet onion, thinly sliced
8 cups bone broth, chicken
1 large carrot, diced
2 ears organic corn, kernels sliced off (or 1 can organic canned corn, drained and rinsed)
4 cups chicken, shredded
1 can black or pinto beans, rinsed
1 red bell pepper, seeded and chopped
1 bunch cilantro, chopped
1 avocado, sliced
3 green onions, chopped
1 bag organic corn tortilla chips
¼ teaspoon cumin
¼ teaspoon paprika
salt and pepper to taste

Heat oil in small skillet over high heat. Add onion and season with salt and pepper. Sauté the onion for 10 minutes; allowing the edges to blacken slightly. Heat bone broth in large pot over medium heat. Add carrot, corn, beans, sautéed onion, and bell pepper. Bring to a low boil and cover. Simmer for 20 minutes. Add shredded chicken and return cover. Continue to boil for 2-3 minutes and then remove from heat. Salt and pepper to taste. Place the desired amount of tortilla chips (crush with your hand) in each bowl. Using a ladle spoon soup into individual bowls. Top with cilantro, avocado, and green onion. Serve hot and enjoy!

Pumpkin and Butternut Squash Soup
Serves 6-8

1 (15 ounce) can organic coconut milk
1 (15 ounce) can organic pumpkin puree
1 (10 ounce) bag organic riced cauliflower
2-pound bag cut butternut squash, 32 ounces
2 tablespoons butter or ghee
1 teaspoon kosher salt
⅛ teaspoon pepper
¼ teaspoon nutmeg
¼ teaspoon coriander

Toppings (choose 1-3)
pecans
dried cherries
golden raisins
cinnamon
raw honey
paprika
apples, cut into small cubes

Place all ingredients in an Instant pot and stir with a wooden spoon to combine. Seal lid and set to Soup. After the pressure naturally releases, use an immersion blender to puree the soup until it is smooth. Garnish with desired topping (s).

If using a crock pot, cook on low for 8 hours or on high for 4 hours and then use the immersion blender to puree.

Broccoli Spinach Soup
Serves 6

2 tablespoons coconut oil
¼ red onion, chopped
2 cloves garlic, minced
4 cups broccoli florets
4 cups spinach or chard
¼ cup cilantro
3 cups bone broth, chicken
¼ cup coconut cream
½ teaspoon cumin
½ teaspoon kosher salt
½ teaspoon pepper

Press sauté button and add oil and onion to Instant pot, sauté for 2 minutes. Turn off sauté and add remaining ingredients, stir to mix. Place lid on securely and press Soup. When it's done cooking carefully preform a quick release by turning the vent to the open position. Remove lid and use an immersion blender to puree content to your desired consistency. Option- top with seeds and a dollop of coconut cream.

If using a crock pot, sauté onion on the stove, then add to slow cooker and cook on low for 8 hours or on high for 4 hours.

Bone Broth

12 cups filtered water
1.5 pounds' chicken bones and gizzards
2 carrots
2 stalks celery
1 cup parsley
1 tablespoon Bragg's apple cider vinegar
2 bay leaves
3 sprigs thyme
1 onion, peeled and quartered
3 cloves garlic, smashed
1 teaspoon fresh ginger, peeled
1 teaspoon fresh turmeric, peeled
¼ teaspoon paprika
1 ½ teaspoons kosher salt
1 tablespoon black peppercorn

Place all ingredients in a slow cooker and cook on low for 24 hours. When done skim the fat off the top. Strain the broth using a cheesecloth or fine- mesh sieve. Store in mason jars for up to 2 weeks in the refrigerator or place in a container and freeze for up to 6 months.

Personal note - I drink 1-2 cups of bone broth each day because it supports digestion and immune function. Avoid if you have histamine intolerance.

Hummus

Avocado Cilantro Hummus
Serves 6

1 (15 ounce) can chickpeas, drained and rinsed or 1.5 cups cauliflower rice
¼ cup cilantro
½ avocado or ½ cup broccoli puree
1 to 2 cloves garlic, minced
1 tablespoon tahini
½ teaspoon salt
¼ cup olive oil
3 tablespoons water
1 teaspoon lemon juice (optional)
salt and pepper to taste

Place chickpeas, avocado, cilantro, garlic, tahini, salt, and the lemon juice in a blender or food processor. Pulse to blend and slowly add in olive oil. Add in water and continue mixing until smooth. If too thick, you can add additional oil until desired consistency - salt and pepper to taste.

Classic Hummus

Serves 6

1 (12 ounce) bag riced cauliflower
3 tablespoons extra virgin olive oil
2 tablespoons tahini
2 tablespoons water
1 to 2 cloves garlic, minced
½ teaspoon salt
½ teaspoon cumin
salt and pepper to taste

Add ingredients to blender or food processor and blend until smooth. Season with salt and pepper to taste. Store in airtight container and place in the refrigerator until ready to serve.

Beet Hummus

Serves 6

1 small roasted beet or ½ cup frozen beets, thawed
3 tablespoons avocado oil
1 (15 ounce) can chickpeas, drained and rinsed
¼ cup tahini
2 medium garlic cloves, minced
1 teaspoon ground coriander
1 teaspoon lemon juice
salt and pepper to taste

Heat oven to 400°F. Line a baking sheet with foil. To roast a fresh beet, peel and slice, then drizzle the beets with 1 tablespoon avocado oil and bake for 25-30 minutes. After the beet has cooled (or frozen beets have thawed), put into the food processor and blend. Add the remaining ingredients except for the oil and blend until smooth. Scrape down the sides of the bowl then blend again as you slowly drizzle in the remaining avocado oil. Season with salt and pepper to taste. Store in an airtight container for up to 7 days and enjoy with raw veggies.

Salads

Hummus Salad Dressing
Serves 4

1/3 cup classic hummus (page 54)
1 garlic clove, minced
2 teaspoons dried herbs of your choice
1 teaspoon lemon or lemon extract
2 teaspoons water
1 tablespoon olive oil
pinch of black pepper

Place all ingredients in a Mason jar or small carafe. Cover with a lid and shake to mix. Serve immediately and store the extra in the fridge for up to 7 days.

Watermelon Mint Salad
Serves 2

Salad
4 cups mixed greens
½ cup fresh mint leaves, chopped
2 cups fresh watermelon, cubed
2 teaspoons pine nuts
2 ounces feta or vegan cheese (optional)

Dressing
2 tablespoons extra virgin olive oil
1 teaspoon lemon extract
2 teaspoons water
1 teaspoon honey
1 teaspoon scallions, minced
salt and pepper to taste

Toss mixed greens, mint, watermelon, and feta together in a large bowl. In a small bowl, whisk together lemon extract, honey, and scallions, then slowly pour in the olive oil as you whisk. Lightly drizzle salad mixture with dressing and toss to mix. Salt and pepper to taste and serve immediately.

Sweet Potato Quinoa Salad
Serves 2

Salad
1 medium sweet potato
1 tablespoon extra-virgin olive oil
1 cup cooked quinoa
4 cups mixed greens
½ cup organic raisins
¼ cup pecans, chopped

Dressing
4 tablespoons classic hummus (page 54)
1 garlic clove, minced
1 tablespoon 100% maple syrup
1 teaspoon dried oregano
1 teaspoon dried basil
1 teaspoon lemon or lemon extract
2 teaspoons water
1 tablespoon olive oil
pinch of black pepper

Preheat the oven to 425° F. Prepare the quinoa according to the directions on the package. Dice the sweet potato, and place on a greased baking sheet and drizzle with oil. Roast for 15 minutes, stir and roast another 5-10 minutes or until tender.

Make the dressing by combining all the ingredients in a medium bowl, whisking slowly as you pour in the olive oil. In a large bowl, add the greens, sweet potatoes, quinoa, raisins, and pecans. Lightly drizzle the salad with dressing, toss to mix and serve immediately.

Apple Walnut Salad
Serves 2

Salad
4 cups romaine lettuce
2 small apples, thinly sliced
¼ cup walnuts, chopped
2 organic, free-range chicken breasts
½ teaspoon garlic powder
pepper to taste

Dressing
2 tablespoons extra virgin olive oil
1 teaspoon lemon extract
2 teaspoons water
1 tablespoon 100% maple syrup
2 tablespoons organic apple juice

Preheat oven to 375°F. Season chicken breast with garlic powder and black pepper and place on a greased baking dish. Bake for 15-20 minutes or until an internal temperature of 165°F. Let rest for 5 minutes and slice.

Place mixed greens, apples, and walnuts in a large bowl. Make the dressing by combining all the ingredients in a medium bowl, whisking slowly as you pour in the olive oil. Lightly drizzle the salad with dressing, toss to mix, and top with chicken. Serve immediately.

Blueberry Avocado Salad
Serves 2

Salad
4 cups spinach
2 cups blueberries
1 avocado, diced
¼ cup pumpkin seeds, unsalted
2 tablespoons extra virgin olive oil
2 organic, free range chicken breasts
½ teaspoon dried basil
salt and pepper

Dressing
1 tablespoon 100% maple syrup
3 tablespoons blueberry or apple juice
1 teaspoon dried basil
2 tablespoons olive oil

Preheat oven to 375°F. Season chicken breast with basil, salt, and black pepper and place on a greased baking dish. Bake for 15-20 minutes or until an internal temperature of 165°F. Remove from oven and let rest for 5 minutes, then slice. Make the dressing by combining all the ingredients in a medium bowl, whisking slowly as you pour in the olive oil.

Place spinach, blueberries, avocado, and pumpkin seeds in a large bowl. Lightly drizzle the salad with the dressing, toss to mix, then top with the chicken and serve.

Chickpea Summer Salad
Serves 2

Salad
2 cups cooked quinoa
1 cup canned chickpea, rinsed
1 red bell pepper, diced
1 orange bell pepper, diced
1 cucumber, diced
1 cup carrot, sliced
2 tablespoons scallions, sliced

Dressing
1 tablespoon extra-virgin olive oil
4 tablespoons classic hummus (page 54)
1 teaspoon apple or pear juice
2 teaspoons water
1 clove garlic, minced
1 teaspoon dried dill
1 teaspoon dried parsley
salt and pepper to taste

Cook the quinoa according to the package directions and let chill in the fridge. Make the dressing by combining all the ingredients in a medium bowl, whisking slowly as you pour in the olive oil. Combine all the veggies, chickpeas, and quinoa in a medium bowl. Pour dressing over the salad and toss to mix. Cover and chill for at least an hour before serving.

Salmon & Avocado Salad
Serves 2

Salad
2 cups kale, chopped
2 cups Brussels sprouts, shredded
1 cup mushroom, sliced
2 medium radishes, thinly sliced
¼ cup sunflower seeds, roasted & unsalted
2 wild-caught salmon fillets
1 tablespoon fresh basil, chopped
1 teaspoon lemon or lemon extract
2 teaspoons water
½ teaspoon garlic powder
2 tablespoons extra virgin olive oil

Dressing
1 avocado
1 tablespoon extra-virgin olive oil
1 clove of garlic, minced
1 teaspoon lemon or lemon extract
2 teaspoons water
salt and pepper to taste

Place salmon in a medium bowl and season with fresh basil, lemon extract, water, and garlic powder. Let the salmon marinate in the refrigerator for at least 30 minutes (up to 24 hours). In a pan, heat oil over medium heat. Add salmon to the pan and cook on one side for about 2-3 minutes, then flip over and cook for an additional 2-3 minutes or until an internal temperature of 145°F.

Add the kale to a large serving bowl and top with Brussels sprouts, mushrooms, radishes, and sunflower seeds. In a blender or food processor, combine avocado, oil, garlic, lemon extract, salt, and pepper. Blend until smooth (can add more oil if desired). Pour the dressing over the salad and toss to evenly coat. Top with salmon and serve.

Chopped Cauliflower Salad
Serves 2

Salad
1 cup cauliflower florets
1 cup broccoli florets
1 cup cabbage slaw
½ cup carrots, shredded
1 celery stalk, chopped
¼ cup fresh parsley, chopped
3 tablespoons unsalted sunflower seeds
3 tablespoons organic raisins

Dressing
2 tablespoons olive oil
3 tablespoons organic apple juice
1 teaspoon fresh ginger, peeled and grated
1 tablespoon honey
salt and pepper to taste

Place cauliflower and broccoli in a food processor and process until finely chopped. Make the dressing by combining all the ingredients in a medium bowl, whisking slowly as you pour in the olive oil. Place all of the salad ingredients in a large bowl and toss with the dressing. Enjoy!

Sesame Ginger Salad
Serves 2

Salad
2 cups kale
2 cups cabbage slaw
1 cup carrot, shredded
¼ cup walnuts, chopped
2 wild-caught salmon fillets
½ teaspoon dried ginger
1 tablespoon coconut aminos
2 tablespoons sesame oil

Dressing
2 tablespoons sesame oil
1 tablespoon coconut aminos
1 tablespoon Bragg's apple cider vinegar or apple juice
2 teaspoons sesame seeds
2 teaspoons scallions, minced
1 teaspoon fresh ginger, peeled and grated
1 garlic clove, minced
salt and pepper to taste

Place salmon in a medium bowl and season with dried ginger and coconut aminos. Let the salmon marinate in the refrigerator for at least 30 minutes (up to 24 hours). Heat the oil in a medium pan over medium heat. Add salmon to the pan and cook on one side for about 2-3 minutes, then flip over and cook for an additional 2-3 minutes or until an internal temperature of 145°F.

Place the kale, cabbage, carrots, and walnuts in a large bowl. Make the dressing by combining all the ingredients in a medium bowl, whisking slowly as you pour in the oil. Pour the dressing over the salad and toss to coat evenly. Top with salmon and serve immediately.

Maple Pear Salad
Serves 2

Salad
4 cups mixed greens
2 small pears, thinly sliced
¼ cup walnuts, chopped
2 ounces feta or vegan cheese (optional)

Dressing
1 tablespoon extra-virgin olive oil
1 tablespoon 100% maple syrup
3 tablespoons organic apple juice
salt and pepper to taste

Place mixed greens, pears, walnuts and feta in a large bowl. Make the dressing by combining all the ingredients in a small bowl, whisking slowly as you pour in the olive oil. Lightly drizzle the salad with dressing, toss to mix, and serve immediately.

Snow Pea Salad
Serves 2

Salad
1 bunch microgreens
6 ounces of snow peas, trimmed
1 cucumber, thinly sliced
6 radishes, thinly sliced

Dressing
1 tablespoon apple juice
1 teaspoon sesame seed oil
2 teaspoons coconut aminos
¼ teaspoon honey
salt and pepper to taste

Whisk salad dressing ingredients together and set aside. Bring 2 cups water to boil. Add snow peas and a dash of salt and boil for 2 minutes, then drain. Allow snow peas to cool, and then toss microgreens, snow peas, cucumber, and radishes together in a bowl. Toss with dressing to mix and enjoy.

Main Courses

Pesto with Zucchini Pasta
Serves 2-3

2 cups fresh basil, stems removed
1 cup spinach or chard, chard stems removed
2 cloves garlic, minced
1 teaspoon lemon juice (optional)
½ teaspoon kosher salt
2 tablespoons pine nuts
½ cup extra virgin olive oil
1 bag zoodles (fresh zucchini noodles) or make your own (see below). You can also use egg noodles.

Place all ingredients (except zucchini) into a food processor and blend until smooth. Set in the fridge and allow it to cool. Prepare noodles according to directions on the bag (If making your own see Zoodles recipe below). Place cooked noodles in a bowl and toss with pesto sauce.

Zoodles
Serves 2

1 large zucchini
1 tablespoon avocado oil
salt and pepper to taste

If you want to make your own zucchini noodles (zoodles), simply cut off the ends of the zucchini and place it on a spiralizer. Turn the knob to spin. You can also use a julienne peeler to slice the zucchini then pull the strands apart with your fingers. Heat the oil in saucepan over medium heat. Once the oil is hot, add zucchini noodles, season with salt and fresh pepper, and sauté for 2-3 minutes. Remove from heat and toss with pesto sauce.

Baked Garlic and Sage Chicken
Serves 4

4 bone-in chicken breasts
2 tablespoons avocado oil
6 cloves garlic, minced
4 tablespoons fresh sage, chopped
1 teaspoon salt
¼ teaspoon freshly ground pepper

Preheat the oven to 425°F. Line a baking dish with unbleached parchment paper. In a small bowl, mix the oil, garlic, and sage together. Rub the chicken with the mixture making sure to coat it evenly, including getting under the skin. Place breasts on lined baking dish, skin side up, and bake for 10 minutes. Reduce heat to 350°F and bake for an additional 30 minutes or until an internal temperature of 165°F. Serve with sprouted rice and steamed veggies.

Hummus Marinade with Lamb

Serves 2-3
by Victor Bolek

½ pounds pasture-raised grass-fed lamb leg steak
¼ cup avocado oil
1 teaspoon fresh or dried rosemary
1 teaspoon fresh or dried thyme
½ teaspoon paprika
⅛ teaspoon cumin
2 tablespoons Avocado and Cilantro Hummus (page 52)

Mix oil, rosemary, thyme, paprika, cumin, and hummus together in a bowl. Pour marinade over the meat, making sure to cover all of it. Cover and refrigerate for up to 8 hours.

Remove meat from marinade and place on a plate, then discard the marinade. Preheat grill for high heat, and cook steaks about 5 minutes on each side for medium-well done or until an internal temperature of 140°F.

Sweet & Salty Tacos
Serves 3-4

1 sweet potato, peeled and chopped
½ small sweet onion, chopped
6 slices organic, pasture and nitrate-free bacon
1 ½ pound chicken thighs (boneless and skinless), chopped
1 teaspoon kosher salt
¼ teaspoon paprika
⅛ teaspoon garlic powder
½ teaspoon freshly ground course pepper
1 tablespoon cilantro stems, finely chopped
1 head bib lettuce
1 avocado, thinly sliced (optional)
1 bunch cilantro, chopped

Mix salt, paprika, garlic powder, and pepper together in a bowl and set aside. In a large skillet over medium heat sauté onion, bacon, and potato until onions and potato are tender, about 10 minutes. Add chicken thighs, seasoning, and cilantro stems and continue to cook until chicken is cooked through, about 5-7 minutes. To make the tacos fill one piece of lettuce with the desired amount of chicken, two slices of avocado, and top with cilantro.

Creamy Butternut Squash Pasta
Serves 2

2 tablespoons ghee
3 cloves garlic, minced
½ cup bone broth, chicken
¼ cup coconut cream
1 tablespoon arrowroot starch
2 tablespoons parsley, chopped
salt and pepper to taste
1 package butternut squash noodles
1 tablespoon avocado oil

In a non-stick pan, heat 1 tablespoon of avocado oil over medium heat. Add the butternut squash noodles and sauté them gently for 8-10 minutes. Turn off heat and set aside. In a small bowl whisk together cream, broth, and arrowroot.

In a saucepan, heat ghee over medium heat and sauté garlic for 1 minute. Add sauce to the pan and let simmer for 5 minutes stirring occasionally. Stir in the parsley. Salt and pepper to taste, and allow to cook for 2 minutes, then remove from heat. Pour over pasta and serve. Garnish with fresh chopped parsley.

Chicken Flautas
Serves 2

1 package cassava flour tortillas
1.5 cups shredded chicken
½ cup crumbled feta cheese made with sheep's milk (more for topping)
1 teaspoon gluten-free flour
1 cup iceberg lettuce, shredded
2 to 3 tablespoons avocado oil

In a small bowl, mix the flour and a little water together to form a paste. Take one tortilla (to soften tortillas and make them pliable you can heat in the microwave for 15-20 seconds) and fill with two large spoons full of chicken and add desired amount of cheese (don't overstuff). Roll tightly to make a neat cylinder and secure with paste so that flauta is glued together. Continue rolling remaining flautas.

Heat oil in a non-stick pan over medium-high heat, making sure the oil coats the bottom of the pan. Add the flautas a few at a time and fry on one side for 2-3 minutes until golden brown. Using tongs, turn and cook the other side for another 2-3 minutes. Drain on paper towels, then split between two plates and top with shredded lettuce and cheese.

Note - You can also omit the cheese or substitute with vegan cream cheese, and they will still taste delicious.

Lettuce Wrapped Subs

Serves 1

½ head iceberg lettuce, cored and outer leaves removed
2 slices organic turkey
2 slices organic ham
2 strips organic bacon, cooked and cut in half
2 tablespoons hummus (page 52)
¼ cucumber, peeled and cut julienne
½ avocado, thinly sliced
handful of sprouts
1-piece unbleached parchment paper, 14 x 14 inches

Lay parchment paper down on the counter. Layer 6-7 pieces of lettuce about 10" x 10" on top. Spread hummus in the middle of the lettuce. Layer with turkey, ham, bacon, cucumber, sprouts, and avocado. Use the parchment paper to roll the lettuce as tightly as you can, making sure to tuck the ends of the wraps towards the middle. When completely wrapped, roll the remainder of the parchment paper around the lettuce tightly. Using a knife cut through the middle of the wrap.

Vegetarian Spring Rolls
Serves 2-3

1 package rice paper wrappers
1 cup carrots, julienned
1 cup purple cabbage, shredded
1 cup cucumber, julienned
1 cup jicama, julienned
1 bunch cilantro, large stems removed
1 large avocado, sliced (optional)
1 large yellow bell pepper, julienned
1 cup rice noodles, cooked (optional)

Nut sauce
¼ cup almond butter
¼ cup canned coconut cream
1 tablespoon coconut aminos
¼ teaspoon roasted sesame oil
¼ teaspoon ginger, grated
1 clove garlic, minced

Place all ingredients for the nut sauce in a food processor and blend until smooth. Set aside. To prep the rolls, fill a bowl with warm water and soak one rice paper at a time until it becomes soft, about 10-15 seconds, making sure to flip over halfway through. Place the paper onto a clean surface such as a counter or a cutting board.

To fill, add veggies starting at the bottom 1/3 of the paper and distribute evenly. Don't overstuff and make sure to leave enough room on all sides to wrap up. Pull the bottom (the part closest to you) of the rice paper wrapper up and over the filling, tucking it under a little bit to pull the ingredients closer together. Gently pull the left side of the wrapper over the middle, and then the right, to close up the ends of the roll. Roll it up away from you, continuing to gently tuck the filling in tighter as you go. Cut in half and serve with dipping sauce.

Herb Roasted Chicken

Serves 4

4 to 5-pound whole organic, free-range chicken, giblets removed
1 to 2 tablespoons avocado oil
4 cloves garlic
1 onion, quartered
1 tablespoon fresh or dried thyme
1 tablespoon fresh or dried rosemary
1 ½ tablespoons kosher salt
1 teaspoon pepper
½ teaspoon garlic powder
¼ cup bone broth, chicken

Heat the oven to 450°F. Clean out cavity of chicken and place inside a deep baking pan, breast side up. In small bowl mix thyme, rosemary, salt, pepper, and garlic powder together. Add the oil to the seasoning mix to form a paste and rub over the entire chicken, including under the skin. Stuff the cavity with onion and garlic. Tie legs together with string and tuck wing tips in. Pour broth into the bottom of the pan. Place chicken in oven and roast at 450°F for 30 minutes. Reduce temperature to 400°F and continue cooking for 30 minutes or until thermometer reads 165°F. Remove from the oven, tent with foil, and let stand 10 minutes before serving.

Sheppard's Pie
Serves 5

Mashed Potatoes
1 ½ pound Yukon Gold Potatoes, peeled and halved (can substitute with 1 package cauliflower rice)
½ cup Cashew Unsweetened Cultured Beverage (or cashew milk)
2 tablespoons raw butter or ghee
salt and pepper to taste

Meat and Veggie Filling
2 tablespoons coconut oil
1 small sweet onion, diced
3 cloves garlic, minced
2 cobs organic corn, kernels removed (or 1 can organic corn, drained)
½ cup fresh peas
1 cup carrots diced
2 tablespoons fresh parsley, chopped
1 to 2 teaspoons fresh or dried rosemary
1 to 2 teaspoons fresh or dried thyme
1 ½ pounds organic grass-fed ground beef or lamb
1 tablespoon gluten-free flour
1 cup bone broth
1 tablespoon kosher salt
¾ teaspoon pepper

Cover potatoes with water and bring to a boil. Reduce heat to a low boil and add ¼ teaspoon of salt to the water. Boil potatoes for 12-15 minutes or until they are tender and cooked, then drain the water and add butter and milk. Using a handheld mixer whip ingredient together until smooth. Salt and pepper to taste and set aside. Heat oven to 400°F. In a large skillet heat oil over medium-high heat. Add onion, carrots, corn, and peas and sauté for 10 minutes. Add meat and garlic. Break up meat and stir to combine, season with salt and pepper. Brown beef about 5 minutes and then stir in the broth, flour, parsley, rosemary, and thyme. Bring to a boil then reduce heat to simmer and cover. Cook for 7-8 minutes, and then remove from heat and place mixture in a baking dish. Top with mashed potatoes and smooth over them using the bottom of a large spoon. Bake for 20 minutes. Let the dish cool for 10 minutes and serve.

Mashed Chickpea Sandwich
Serves 2

1 can organic chickpeas, rinsed or 1 can tuna in water, drained
3 tablespoons cilantro
1 tablespoon olive oil
½ teaspoon cumin
¼ teaspoon kosher salt
¼ teaspoon pepper
½ Meyer lemon, juiced (optional)
2 handfuls microgreens
½ cucumber, chopped
½ carrot, shredded
4 slices of bread

Place chickpeas, cilantro, oil, lemon, cumin, and salt in a food processor or blender and gently blend about 5-10 seconds. Transfer to a bowl and stir in cucumbers. Season with salt and pepper to taste. You can add more oil as needed if the mash is too dry. Toast the bread. To serve, spread chickpea mash on to a slice of bread and top with microgreens and carrots. Top with the second slice of bread. Cut sandwich in half and enjoy!

Best and Easiest Pot Roast Recipe Ever
Serves 6

3.5 to 4-pound grass-fed chuck roast 1 sweet onion, sliced
3 cloves garlic
1 bay leaf
1 teaspoon avocado oil
1 cup bone broth
1 tablespoon kosher salt
½ teaspoon pepper
dash of red wine vinegar
1 large carrot, roughly chopped
24 ounces of potatoes, quartered or halved (fingerling, Yukon, sweet, red)

Place all ingredients in a crockpot, then cover and cook on low for 8 hours or on high for 5 hours. *The secret is in the cut of beef, and high-quality grass- fed beef will taste best.*

Fish

Salmon Lite

Serves 2-3

2 small wild caught salmon fillets
2 tablespoons ghee
2 tablespoons coriander
2 tablespoons nuts (almond, cashew, walnut, macadamia)
2 tablespoons avocado oil
4 tablespoons cilantro
1 bunch asparagus, ends trimmed
salt and pepper to taste

Heat oven to 425°F. Line baking sheet with unbleached parchment paper. Place ghee, coriander, nuts, oil, and cilantro in a food processor, and blend until smooth. Place fish on baking sheet skin side down. Rub mixture onto fish, season with salt and pepper, and bake for 12-15 minutes or until the fish flakes with a fork. Serve warm. Can pair with asparagus, quinoa, or sweet potato.

For the Asparagus, heat ¼ cup water in a pan. Once boiling, add asparagus and cover with a lid. Cook for 3 minutes making sure to turn over halfway through to ensure it cooks evenly. Remove from heat immediately and place on a plate. Drizzle with olive oil, a dash of lemon, and season with kosher salt.

Coconut Macadamia Crusted Mahi Mahi

Serves 2

2 wild-caught Mahi Mahi fillets
2 slices gluten-free bread, toasted
1 cup macadamia nuts
¼ cup unsweetened organic coconut flakes
2 tablespoons coconut flour
¼ cup coconut milk
salt and pepper to taste

Heat oven to 425°F. Line baking sheet with unbleached parchment paper. Place milk in a shallow dish and set aside. In a food processor or blender, pulse macadamia nuts until they are lightly ground. Remove and do the same to the coconut flakes, followed by the toasted bread.

Place nuts in a shallow dish and mix in the breadcrumbs, flour, and coconut. Set aside. Dip fish into milk and then season each side of the fish with salt and pepper. Next, place fish into nut mixture, making sure to gently press nut mixture into each side so that is coats evenly. Place fish on lined baking sheet and bake for 10-15 minutes or until meat is white and flaky. Pair with steamed veggies and sprouted rice.

Honey Glazed Salmon
Serves 2

1/3 cup coconut aminos
1/3 cup organic toasted sesame oil
2 tablespoons raw honey
1 teaspoon fresh ginger, grated
1 tablespoon shallots, minced
4 dashes of ground turmeric
¼ teaspoon vanilla
1 tablespoon avocado oil
2 fillets of wild caught salmon, skin removed (I prefer Alaskan Sockeye)

Place salmon in a zip lock bag or medium bowl. In a small bowl or measuring cup, mix together coconut aminos, sesame oil, honey, ginger, shallots, turmeric, and vanilla. Pour half of the marinade on the salmon and save the other half for later. Let the salmon marinate in the refrigerator for at least 30 minutes.

Heat avocado oil in a pan over medium heat. Add salmon to the pan but discard the used marinade. Cook salmon on one side for about 2-3 minutes, then flip over and cook for an additional 2-3 minutes or until cooked through. Remove salmon from the pan and pour the remaining marinade in the pan and reduce (about 2-3 minutes). Pour marinade over fillets and serve with a side of veggies, sprouted quinoa, or over a bed of lettuce.

Sides

Warm Dandelion Greens
Serves 2

1 bunch dandelion greens, rinsed and trimmed
2 tablespoons olive oil
dash of lemon
salt and pepper to taste

Bring 5 cups of water to boil. Submerge the greens in the water and let cook for 5-7 minutes, or until tender. Drain the water (option- you can save the water and season with salt and pepper and drink it as a tea). Allow to cool for 3 minutes, then drizzle oil over greens and season with salt and pepper. You can add a dash or two of Meyer lemon if you are able to tolerate it. Enjoy the greens warm or store in the refrigerator for up to three days.

Roasted Chickpeas
Serves 6

2 cans chickpeas, drained and rinsed
2 tablespoons avocado oil
1 teaspoon garlic powder
1 teaspoon fresh or dried dill

Preheat the oven to 400°F. Dry the chickpeas with a towel or pat to dry. In a medium bowl, toss the chickpeas with oil. Transfer to a baking sheet and bake for 20-30 minutes or until golden brown. Stir or shake the pan every 10 minutes. Remove from the oven, toss with the seasonings, and let cool for 5-10 minutes. Enjoy ½ cup as a snack or on top of salads! Keep in a container (not airtight) at room temperature for up to 5 days or in the freezer for up to 1 month.

Wilted Chard with Bacon

Serves 2

3 slices organic pasture-raised and nitrate-free bacon, chopped
1 tablespoon shallot, minced
6 cups swiss chard, chopped
salt and pepper to taste

In a skillet over medium-high heat, sauté bacon and shallot for 3-4 minutes. Add the swiss chard and sauté for another 3-4 minutes or until greens are wilted. Season with salt and pepper and serve.

Roasted Brussels Sprouts with Bacon

Serves 4

1-pound Brussels sprouts
2 tablespoons ghee, melted
2 cloves garlic, minced
1 tablespoon shallot, minced
1 teaspoon maple syrup
¼ teaspoon freshly ground pepper
4 slices organic pasture-raised and nitrate-free bacon, chopped

Preheat oven to 400°F. Line a baking sheet with unbleached parchment paper. Trim the ends of the Brussel sprouts and remove any old outer leaves, then cut them in half. In a bowl, whisk together ghee, maple syrup, shallots, garlic, and pepper. Add Brussels sprouts and bacon and toss them together until coated.

Arrange them in a single layer on the baking sheet and bake for 25-30 minutes making sure to rotate halfway through. They will be tender on the inside and crispy on the outside. Season with salt and pepper to taste, and let cool for 5 minutes, then serve.

Mango Avocado Salad
Makes 2 cups

1 mango, peeled, pitted, and cubed
1 avocado, peeled, pitted, and cubed
3 tablespoons red onion, finely chopped
¼ cup cilantro, chopped
½ teaspoon kosher salt
1 tablespoon extra-virgin olive oil
½ teaspoon lemon juice (optional)

Gently toss all ingredients together in a bowl and serve immediately. Enjoy with organic corn tortilla chips or serve with fish or tacos.

Baked Kale Chips
Serves 4

1 head kale, washed and dried
2 tablespoons avocado oil
½ teaspoon kosher sea salt
⅛ teaspoon garlic powder
⅛ teaspoon smoked or regular paprika (optional)

Heat oven to 300°F. Cover 2 baking sheets with unbleached parchment paper. Using a knife, remove the leaves from the ribs and discard the ribs. Cut leaves into 2-inch pieces. Place kale in a bowl and toss with oil. Use hands to make sure that each leaf is coated. Split the kale between the baking sheets and spread out in a single layer. Sprinkle with salt, garlic powder, and paprika. Bake for 15 minutes or until lightly browned.

Sheet Roasted Veggies
Serves 4-5

2 cups broccoli florets
3 cups butternut squash, chopped
½ sweet onion, roughly chopped and separated
2 cups cauliflower florets
2 medium purple or white sweet potatoes, washed and cubed
1 yellow bell pepper, seeded and diced
2 cups Brussels sprouts, sliced
2 tablespoons avocado oil
2 teaspoons kosher sea salt
1 teaspoon Italian Seasoning (optional)

Preheat the oven to 425°F. Cut the veggies into small pieces. Combine veggies in a bowl and toss with oil making sure to coat all the vegetables lightly. Season with salt and Italian Seasoning if using. Place veggies on a nonstick baking sheet and bake for 25 minutes or until the veggies are tender and lightly browned.

Baked Sweet Potato
Serves 2

2 large white sweet potatoes
1 teaspoon cinnamon
2 teaspoons coconut sugar
1 teaspoon ghee or raw butter
pinch of salt
1 tablespoon pecans, chopped

Heat oven to 350°F. Line baking sheet with unbleached parchment paper. Pierce each sweet potato twice with a fork. Place on a baking tray and bake until soft (about 45 minutes). Cut potatoes lengthwise and lightly mash meat with a fork, then add butter, salt, cinnamon, and sugar and mix with potato using the fork. Add pecans and enjoy!

Roasted Carrots with Rosemary

Serves 4

1-pound carrots, peeled and cut into 2 x ¼-inch matchsticks
2-3 cloves garlic, minced
2 teaspoons fresh rosemary, chopped
2 teaspoons avocado oil
¼ teaspoon kosher salt

Preheat oven to 400°F. Line pan with unbleached parchment paper. Place carrots, rosemary, and garlic in bowl, and toss with oil using your hands to make sure you coat carrots evenly. Spread carrots out on baking dish and season with salt. Bake for 18-20 minutes or until tender.

Sweets

No Bake Apple Pie Bites
Serves 12-16

½ cup gluten free oats
½ cup ground flaxseed
½ cup almond butter
1 cup dried apples or pears
1/2 cup 100% maple syrup
½ teaspoon apple pie spice
½ teaspoon cinnamon
1 teaspoon pure vanilla extract

Blend all ingredients in a food processor until mixture comes together. Cover and let chill in the refrigerator for 30 minutes. Once chilled, roll into balls that are approximately 1 inch in diameter. Store in an airtight container and keep in the refrigerator for up to 1 week or in the freezer for up to one month.

Chocolate Almond Nice Cream
Serves 2

3 ripe bananas, sliced and frozen
¼ cup unsweetened nut milk
2 tablespoons almond butter
¼ teaspoon pure vanilla extract
3 tablespoons carob powder

Place bananas, milk, almond butter and vanilla into a food processor. Pulse until smooth (pausing to stir/scrape the sides as needed). Add in carob powder and pulse again. Serve immediately or transfer to a container and freeze for at least 30 minutes before scooping into a bowl. Enjoy!

Berry Nice Cream
Serves 2

3 ripe bananas, sliced and frozen
¼ cup unsweetened nut milk
1 cup frozen berries (of your choice)
¼ teaspoon pure vanilla extract

Place bananas, milk, and vanilla into a food processor. Pulse until smooth (pausing to stir/scrape the sides as needed). Add in frozen berries and pulse again. Serve immediately or transfer to a container and freeze for at least 30 minutes before scooping into a bowl. Enjoy!

Avocado Chocolate Mousse

Serves 2

1 ripe avocado
¼ cup carob powder
¼ cup unsweetened nut milk
¼ teaspoon vanilla extract
2 tablespoons 100% pure maple syrup

Cut the avocado in half, remove the pit, and scoop out. Cut the avocado flesh into large chunks. Place all ingredients in a food processor and blend until completely smooth. Adjust milk, carob powder, or maple syrup as needed to taste. Transfer to serving glasses (i.e. Mason jar) and refrigerate for 30-60 minutes. Serve cold.

Baked Pears
Serves 2

2 pears, cored and chopped
½ teaspoon cinnamon
drizzle of honey (optional)

Preheat oven to 350°F. Place pears in small baking dish and bake for 15-20 minutes or until soft. Remove from the oven and sprinkle with the cinnamon and add a drizzle of honey.

Apple Crisp
Serves 4

Toppings
3 tablespoons almond or oat flour
¼ cup gluten free old-fashioned oats
3 tablespoons dark brown coconut sugar
¼ cup chopped almonds
⅛ teaspoon ground cinnamon
2 tablespoons cold ghee, diced into small cubes

Crisp
3 crisp Gala or Fuji apples, peeled, cored and thinly sliced
2 tablespoons maple syrup
½ teaspoon apple pie spice
2 teaspoons pure vanilla extract

Preheat the oven to 350°F and grease a small baking pan with avocado oil. In a mixing bowl, add the topping ingredients mixing together with your hands, and place in the fridge. In a separate mixing bowl, add crisp ingredients then stir to combine and let sit for 10 minutes.

Add the crisp ingredients to the baking dish and spread the topping mixture over the apples. Bake for 45 minutes or until golden brown. Remove from the oven and let cool for 10 minutes. Serve warm and enjoy!

Coconut Peach Parfait
Serves 4

1 cup coconut milk yogurt
1 teaspoon maple syrup
1 cup peach, cubed
1 cup gluten-free granola
cinnamon

To make the parfait, layer ¼ cup yogurt in a Mason jar or water glass, then add ¼ cup peaches, ¼ teaspoon maple syrup, and ¼ cup granola. Repeat, making four layers. Top with cinnamon.

Pumpkin Pie Chia Pudding
Serves 2

½ cup canned pumpkin
1 cup unsweetened nut milk
¼ teaspoon pumpkin pie spice
½ teaspoon cinnamon
1 teaspoon vanilla extract
1 tablespoon 100% maple syrup
¼ cup chia seeds
¼ cup roasted almonds

Mix the pumpkin, milk, spices, vanilla, maple syrup & seeds in a Mason jar until blended. Place in the fridge overnight. When ready to eat, top with roasted almonds and enjoy!

Berry Chia Parfait
Serves 2

¼ cup chia seeds
¾ cup unsweetened nut milk
¼ cup coconut water
pinch of sea salt
1 tablespoon pure maple syrup
⅛ teaspoon vanilla extract
⅛ teaspoon cinnamon
½ up raspberries
½ cup blueberries
¼ cup strawberries, sliced
4 mint leaves

Mix the seeds, milk, water, salt, syrup, vanilla, and cinnamon, in a Mason jar until blended. Gently stir in ¼ cup raspberries and ¼ cup blueberries and cover. Place in the fridge overnight. When ready to eat, stir, and top with the remaining blueberries and raspberries, plus the strawberries and mint leaves. Enjoy!

Strawberry Pureed Yogurt
Serves 2

1 cup fresh strawberries, tops removed
1 cup plain yogurt (I prefer Kite Hill plain almond milk)
¼ cup granola, gluten-free
handful of blueberries

Place strawberries in a food processor and blend until smooth. Divide the puree between two bowls and top each with the yogurt. Sprinkle the granola and blueberries on top and enjoy!

Note: You can use blueberries, peaches, or pears if you are intolerant to strawberries. If fruit is not sweet enough you can drizzle a little honey on top.

IC Diet Protocol

Acai - WT
Allspice - WT
Almond Extract - BF
Almonds - BF (soak 24 hours beforehand, rinse)
Aloe - WT
Amaranth - WT
Anise - BF
Apples - BF (Fuji, Gala, Pink Lady)
Apricots - WT
Arrowroot Flour - BF
Artichokes - BF
Asparagus - BF
Autolyzed yeast - Avoid
Avocado - BF
Bacon - BF (organic, pasture-raised, nitrate-free)
Baking Powder - BF (aluminum-free)
Baking Soda - BF (Bob's Red Mill)
Banana's - WT
Basil - BF
Beans - BF (soak 24 hours beforehand, rinse or buy sprouted)
Beef - BF (grass-fed, grass-finished, organic, exotic, wild game)
Beer - Avoid
Bell Pepper - BF
Berries - BF (blueberries), WT (raspberries, strawberries, blackberries)
Blueberries - BF
Bone Broth - BF (organic or homemade)
Bouillon - Avoid
Bread - BF (gluten-free *Bakehouse Canyon Ancient Grains), Avoid (gluten and dairy)
Broccoli - BF
Brussels sprouts - BF
Butter - BF (Ghee, vegan), WT (raw, Irish)
Buttermilk - Avoid, WT (homemade using raw milk, substitute with cultured cashew milk)
Cabbage - BF
Cacao - Avoid
Cantaloupe - WT
Caraway seeds - BF
Carob - WT

Carrots - BF
Cauliflower - BF
Cayenne - Avoid
Celery - BF
Celery Seed - WT
Cereal - BF (gluten-free, dairy-free, Non-GMO, No artificial sweeteners or refined sugar)
Cheese - WT (feta, raw, goat, sheep, almond), Avoid (conventional)
Cherries - WT, Avoid (sour cherries)
Chia Seeds - WT
Chicken - BF (organic free-range)
Chili peppers - Avoid
Chili powder - Avoid
Chips - BF (organic corn or potato), Avoid (artificial flavors and cooking oils)
Cilantro - BF
Cinnamon - BF
Citrus fruits - WT (Meyer lemon, citrus peel), Avoid (grapefruit, orange, limes, tangerines)
Cloves - WT
Coconut - BF
Coffee - Avoid, WT (chicory)
Cocoa - Avoid
Coriander - BF
Corn - BF (organic Non-GMO)
Cornstarch - WT (organic, Non-GMO)
Cottage cheese - Avoid
Cranberry - Avoid
Cream cheese - avoid, WT (almond or nut based non-dairy)
Creamer - Avoid, WT (plant-based)
Cucumber - BF
Cumin - WT
Curry - Avoid, WT (yellow)
Dates - BF (organic, dried), WT (Medjool)
Deli meats - BF (organic, nitrate-free), Avoid (processed)
Dill - BF
Dried fruits - WT (apple, peach, apricots, prunes, raisins, cherries, figs)
Eggnog - BF (homemade with nut milk)
Eggplant - WT
Eggs - BF (organic free-range)
Fennel - BF
Fermented Foods - WT
Figs - WT
Fish - BF (wild caught), WT (anchovies, canned tuna in water)

Flaxseed oil - WT
Flour - BF (almond, arrowroot, buckwheat, cassava, chickpea, coconut, organic rice, organic sprouted corn, Tiger nut), Bob's Red Mill All-Purpose, WT (Pamela's gluten- free). Avoid (gluten)
Food coloring- Avoid, BF (from fruits or vegetables only)
Garlic - BF, WT (garlic salt)
Gelatin - BF (grass-fed, pasture-raised)
Ginger - BF
Grains - (organic sprouted and gluten-free. Amaranth, Millet, Quinoa, Teff, Rice, Polenta, Sorghum). Avoid (gluten)
Graham Crackers - WT (gluten-free)
Grapes - WT
Green beans - BF
Guava - WT
Horseradish - Avoid
Hot dogs - BF (organic grass-fed), Avoid traditional
Ice cream - BF (plant based non-dairy), Avoid (dairy)
Juice - BF (pear, blueberry, fresh pressed), WT (apple, mango, low-acid orange)
Kiwi - Avoid
Kombucha - WT (no more than 4 ounces per day if tolerable)
Lamb - BF (grass-fed and pasture raised)
Lard - Avoid, substitute with Palm Shortening
Leeks - WT
Lemons - WT (Meyer lemons, lemon zest)
Lemon extract - WT
Lettuce - BF
Licorice- WT
Liquor - Avoid
Liver - BF
Mango - WT
Maple Syrup - BF (organic, 100% pure)
Marjoram - BF
Mayonnaise - WT (homemade, vegan, made with avocado oil)
Melons - WT (watermelon, honeydew, cantaloupe)
Milk - BF (nut, oat, coconut, rice), WT (raw, goat, sheep, cashew), Avoid (conventional)
Milkshakes - BF (nut milk based), Avoid (milk/dairy based)
Miso - Avoid (contains MSG and Additives)
Mushrooms - BF
Mustard - WT, Avoid (hot or spicy)
Nectarines - WT
Nut butters - BF (almond), WT (cashew), Avoid (peanut)

Nutmeg - BF
Nutritional yeast - Avoid
Nuts - WT (almond, cashew, pecans, walnut, tiger nut, macadamia, pistachio, hazelnut, brazil (soak for 24 hours beforehand then rinse).
Oatmeal - BF (certified organic, gluten-free, or sprouted gluten-free)
Oil - BF (almond, coconut, extra virgin olive, toasted sesame, sesame, pumpkin, herb-infused). WT (flaxseed, walnut, hemp), Avoid (canola, corn, soy, peanut, vegetable).
Olives – WT
Onion - WT
Onion powder - WT
Orange extract - WT
Oregano - BF
Papaya - WT
Paprika - WT
Parsley - BF
Passion fruit - WT
Pasta - BF (gluten-free, spaghetti squash, egg, quinoa, zucchini, rice)
Peaches - WT
Peanuts – Avoid
Peanut butter – Avoid, BF (Almond)
Pear - BF
Peas - BF
Pepper - WT (Peppercorn white or black)
Persimmon - WT
Pickles - Avoid
Pineapple - Avoid
Pizza - WT (homemade, gluten-free), Avoid (gluten, yeast, dairy, tomato sauce)
Plums - WT
Popcorn - BF (organic sprouted and air popped), Avoid (movie and microwavable)
Poppy seed - BF
Pork - BF (pasture-raised, organic, nitrate-free)
Poultry - BF (organic free-range)
Preservatives - Avoid
Processed meats - BF (pasteurized, organic, nitrate-free) otherwise Avoid
Protein powder - BF (organic, grass-fed, plant-based)
Prunes - WT
Pumpkin - BF
Quinoa - BF (organic sprouted)
Radishes - BF
Raisins - WT
Rhubarb - BF (fresh)

Rice - BF (organic, sprouted)
Rosemary - BF
Rutabaga - BF
Sage - BF
Salt - BF (Kosher, Sea, Himalayan, Celtic)
Sauerkraut - Avoid
Seafood - BF (fresh or wild caught), Avoid (preserved, prepackaged, imitation crab)
Seaweed - BF (snacks, roasted, sheets, Nori)
Seeds - WT (pumpkin, chia, hemp, flaxseed, sunflower, sesame), Avoid (spicy)
Sherbet - Avoid
Shortening - BF (Palm shortening), Avoid (soy, traditional)
Smoked fish - Avoid
Soda - Avoid, WT (sparkling *Izze)
Sorbet - BF (pear, blueberry, coconut), WT (raspberry, mango, peach, blackberry), Avoid (lemon, lime, orange)
Sour cream - Avoid
Soy - WT (organic)
Soy sauce – Avoid, WT (coconut aminos)
Spirulina - BF
Strawberries - WT
Squash - BF
Sweetener - BF (coconut sugar, stevia, 100 % maple syrup, raw honey, Molasses, Monk fruit). Avoid (Splenda, NutraSweet, saccharine, Sweet-n-low, aspartame)
Tahini - WT
Tamari - WT
Tarragon - BF
Teas - BF (licorice, corn silk, roasted dandelion, chamomile, lavender, peppermint, nettle), WT (marshmallow, detox, decaf). Avoid (caffeinated, citrus)
Thyme - BF
Tofu - WT (organic)
Tomatoes - WT (yellow, red heirlooms- seeds removed), Avoid (others)
Tortillas - BF (cassava, Non-GMO corn)
Turkey - BF (organic free-range)
Turmeric - WT
Turnips - BF
Vanilla - BF
Vegetable stock - BF
Vinegar - WT (Apple Cider *Bragg- made without yeast)
Vitamins - BF (A, B1, B2, Methylated B12, D3/K2, E, Omega-3), WT (Vitamin C 'Buffered Ascorbic'), Avoid (B6, Folic acid, vitamin C, synthetic)
Water - BF (filtered, distilled), WT (alkaline)

Watercress - WT
Watermelon - WT
Whipped cream - BF (coconut) otherwise Avoid
Worcestershire sauce - Avoid

BF = Bladder Friendly   WT = Worth Trying

Supplements & Herbs

It is best to begin with one supplement at a time as needed, and we recommend cutting the dose in fourths and adding slowly from there. Allowing the body a week or more to adjust to a new supplement may benefit those sensitive to certain ingredients. Sometimes it takes the immune system time to calm down, so be patient and move slowly. You may find that as you heal, your body can better tolerate specific supplements, so don't be afraid to try again. As with everything, everyone is unique, which means that some people will tolerate certain foods, chemicals, and supplements that others with IC/PBS cannot. We recommend having an open discussion with your medical provider before starting any supplements. *Please see disclaimer.*

Adrenal support - supports optimal stress response and adrenal fatigue, as well as adrenal health and stress hormone production.

Alfalfa Leaf - aids in digestion, cleanses toxins from the body, anti-inflammatory, neutralizes acidity, and is often used to treat urinary problems and muscle spasms.

Aloe Vera - increases the production of GAG molecules in the bladder (wound healing).

Astragalus root - relaxes the bladder and reduces inflammation.

Bromelain – it is anti-microbial & anti-inflammatory. It is effective against Candida overgrowth, inflammation, and soft tissue injuries. Possesses wound healing properties and improves circulation.

Caprylic Acid- beneficial against Candida overgrowth by creating an inhospitable environment for opportunistic yeast.

Collagen - maintains a healthy intestinal barrier. This amino acid supports cellular health and tissue growth and helps repair leaky gut.

Curcumin - controls inflammation and supports immune function.

D-Mannose - treats and prevents UTIs by preventing the bacteria E. coli from attaching to the walls of the urinary tract. D-Mannose provides a preferred surface for bacteria to attach so that they are removed during urination.

Digestive Enzymes - supports digestion and promotes enhanced nutrient bioavailability and absorption.

Digestive Enzymes with HCl - (addresses low stomach acid) enzymes to support the digestion of protein, carbohydrates, fat, fiber, and dairy. Supports optimal gastric pH.

Estroprotect - supports optimal estrogen balance and metabolism.

Flaxseed - is a rich source of healthy fat, antioxidants, and fiber. Improves digestion and cholesterol levels. May decrease bladder inflammation.

Ginger - possesses anti-inflammatory, anti-fungal, and antioxidant properties. Reduces menstrual pain and aids in digestion.

Histazyme - supports the healthy breakdown and digestion of food derived histamine. Note - if you struggle with candida overgrowth or histamine intolerance you may benefit from a low-histamine diet.

Kava root - works quickly to reduce bladder tension and pain.

l-Arginine - opens up blood vessels and increases circulation. 1,500 mg daily has been shown to decrease pain and urgency and improve interstitial cystitis symptoms.

L-glutamine - this nonessential amino acid supports intestinal health and maintains the intestinal barrier.

l-theanine - this amino acid promotes relaxation without drowsiness. Great for those struggling with anxiety or stress.

Lauricidin (Monolaurin) - treats chronic fatigue and boosts the immune system. Potential treatment for Candida albicans/Candida overgrowth.

Liver Support - helps detox and optimize liver function. Crucial for those with IC.

Magnesium L-threonate - supports brain health, cognitive function, and promotes mood balance and sleep.

Methylated B12 - supports methylation, increases energy and red cell production, DNA synthesis and repair, and supports numerous systems in the body.

N-Acetyl-Cysteine (NAC) - a powerful antioxidant that acts as a scavenger of free radicals. It may protect the liver and help prevent bladder damage caused by certain drugs.

Oil of Oregano - an essential oil that is effective against bacterial and fungal infections. It is anti-inflammatory, aids in digestion, and can help balance bacteria - serving as a natural treatment for Candida and SIBO by hindering bacterial replication.

Omega 3 - fatty acids help decrease system-wide inflammation and can help improve autoimmune disease symptoms.

Probiotics - shown to maintain healthy gut barrier function and immunity by promoting microbial diversity and healthy gut bacteria. I highly recommend Megaspore Biotic by Microbiome Labs. This probiotic is 100% spore-based and is well absorbed.

Pumpkin seed oil - effective in wound healing and is an excellent source of antioxidants, zinc, fatty acids, and magnesium.

Quercetin - helps minimize bladder spasms and is effective in reducing IC symptoms.

Reishi mushroom - a fungus/adaptogenic herb with anti-inflammatory properties. It offers protection against inflammation, fatigue, liver disease, allergies & asthma, leaky gut, and autoimmune disorders. Used to increase white blood cell count, fight infection, as well as protect the endocrine system.

Slippery Elm - soothes the lining of the urinary tract.

Turmeric - effective against bladder infections and stops the production of NF kappa-B, a major trigger of bladder inflammation.

Vitamin A - enhances immune function. This "anti-inflammation" vitamin helps to maintain the epithelial and mucous tissue.

Vitamin D3/ K2 - supports skeletal muscle strength and function of the pelvic floor. Maintains immune and neurological function.

Disclaimer

Make sure you consult with your healthcare practitioner before incorporating any supplements. Certain medications may interact with supplements, and some individuals may not be able to tolerate them. Also, seek to find balance here. Do not overload your body with vitamins, which can put too much strain on your system. Add one supplement at a time as needed, and if you find that you are able to tolerate it, add in another one every three days or so. Once you begin to feel better, rotate them, and then seek to reduce usage. Above is merely a list of options, and it is not recommended nor advised that take them all simultaneously. Once you address root causes and feel more balanced, you will only need to support areas where you know you are prone to struggle or are deficient.

Teas for Wellness

Teas (drink 1-2 cups a day)

Chamomile with Lavender - calming; it settles the nervous system when stressed.

Corn Silk - reduces inflammation in the bladder and can help reduce IC symptoms.

Ginger - promotes healthy digestion, reduces inflammation, improves blood circulation, helps relieve menstrual discomfort, relieves nausea, strengthens immunity, and helps alleviate respiratory problems.

Licorice root - Soothes the digestive tract and promotes respiratory health.

Marshmallow Root - promotes wound healing, soothes, and protects mucous membranes.

Milk Thistle - supports liver function and detoxification, protects your bones, and reduces insulin resistance.

Peppermint - alleviates digestive discomfort and soothes the stomach, may have antimicrobial properties, improves sleep, helps relieve headaches and migraines, and ease menstrual cramps.

Red Raspberry leaf - high in magnesium, potassium, iron, and b vitamins. Aids in detoxification. Consult with your doctor first if you are pregnant or nursing.

Roasted Dandelion - detoxifies the liver, acts as a diuretic, full of antioxidants, good for the digestive system.

Slippery Elm Bark - soothes the lining of the urinary tract.

Turmeric - boosts immune function, reduces inflammation, reduces arthritis symptoms, neutralizes free radicals and increases the antioxidant capacity of the body, improves cognitive function, improves mood and sleep, can lower the risk of heart disease, and studies have found that curcumin can reduce the growth of cancerous cells.

Yogi Detox - aids in detoxification, is known to stimulate digestion, and may have a laxative effect.

Note - *start slow and only dip the tea bag twice in the water before consuming tea. At first, certain teas like marshmallow root may irritate the bladder. It is best to start slow and increase from there. The bladder will typically calm down and be better equipped to handle tea, herbs, and supplements when inflammation has decreased.*

About IC Wellness

IC Wellness serves as an online community and resource center for those battling interstitial cystitis and autoimmunity. Founded by author Elisabeth Yaotani, IC Wellness is a place of solace and information. From recipes and blog posts to a store, podcast and IC Forum, we want you to know that we've got you covered.

Diet, lifestyle, and mindset are the three critical areas in managing our lives. A disruption in any of these can cascade into physical as well as emotional difficulties. Navigating these areas alone can be frustrating.

The road to dealing with IC head-on can be a difficult one, and Elisabeth's book reveals how she dealt with this often-debilitating situation and overcame it in:

How I Got My Life Back; My Journey with Interstitial Cystitis

Elisabeth Yaotani has joined forces with nutritionist Brianne Thornton, MS, RD to bring the IC community the support and solutions they deserve. We believe that the foundation of health and wellness exists in diet and lifestyle.

Those who receive personalized nutrition advice are far more likely to have success in overcoming health concerns. Problems such as IC/PBS, SIBO, IBS, candida overgrowth, nutrient deficiencies, digestive issues, and autoimmunity are a daily fight.

Brianne Thornton, MS, RD is trained in integrative and functional nutrition and provides personalized nutrition that identifies and removes barriers to healing. She works with clients to make diet and lifestyle changes that decrease chronic inflammation contributing to illness. To connect with Brianne and learn the process of healing, *visit www.icwellness.org*.

To order Elisabeth's book How I Got My Life Back and start your own journey to health and wellness visit Amazon or www.icwellness.org.

Made in the USA
Las Vegas, NV
30 November 2022

60797127R00077